A Salute to Historic Blacks in the Arts

Copyright © 1990, 1996 by Empak Publishing Company

ISBN 0-922162-8-5 (Volume VIII)
ISBN 0-922162-15-8 (Volume Set)

Library of Congress Cataloging-in-Publication Data

A Salute to Historic Blacks in the Arts.
  p.   cm. – (An Empak "Black history" publication series ; vol. 8)

Publisher and editor: Richard L. Green ; assoc. editors, Melody M. McDowell, Sylvia
Shepherd ; illustration, S. Gaston Dobson. – [Updated ed.]

Summary: Presents biographies of twenty-four black men and women who made
notable contributions in the arts, including Marion Anderson, James Baldwin, Alexander
Dumas, Lorraine Hansberry, Paul Robeson, and Bert Williams.
ISBN 0-922162-08-5

1. Afro-American artists – Biography – Juvenile literature. 2. Afro Americans in art –
Juvenile literature. 3. Afro-American arts – Juvenile literature. [1. Afro-Americans –
Biography. 2. Blacks – Biography.] I. Green, Richard L. II. McDowell, Melody M.
III. Shepherd, Sylvia. IV. Series: Empak "Black history" publication series ; v. 8.

NX512.3.A35S25 1996   95-48500
700'.92'2–dc20   CIP
[B]   AC

A Salute to Historic Blacks in the Arts

EMPAK PUBLISHING COMPANY

Publisher & Editor: Richard L. Green
Assoc. Editors: Melody M. McDowell, Sylvia Shepherd
Researcher: Melody M. McDowell
Production: Dickinson & Associates, Inc.
Illustration: S. Gaston Dobson
Foreword: Empak Publishing Co.

The Negro Artist and the Racial Mountain, The Nation
June 23, 1926

The younger Negro artists who create now intend to express our individual dark-skinned selves without fear or shame. If white people are pleased we are glad. If they are not, it doesn't matter. We know we are beautiful. And ugly, too. The tom-tom cries, and the tom-tom laughs. If colored people are pleased we are glad. If they are not, their displeasure doesn't matter either. We build our temples for tomorrow, strong as we know how, and we stand on top of the mountain free within ourselves.

Langston Hughes

The American Dream Is At the Expense of the American Negro
February, 1965

Until the moment comes when we, the Americans, are able to accept the fact that my ancestors are both black and white, that on that continent we are trying to forge a new identity, that we need each other, that I am not a ward of America, I am not an object of missionary, I am one of the people who built the country ... there is scarcely any hope for the American dream. If the people are denied participation in it, by their very presence they will wreck it.

James Baldwin

A Matter of Color, 1965

The laws which force segregation do not presume the inferiority of a people; they assume an inherent equalness. It is the logic of the lawmakers that if a society does not erect artificial barriers between people at every point of contact, the people might fraternize and give their attention to the genuine, shared problem of the community.

Lorraine Hansberry

CONTENTS

Editor's Note: Due to this booklet's space limitations, some facets an the lives of the above noted Historic Blacks in the Arts have been omitted.

IRA FREDERICK ALDRIDGE
C.1807 - 1867

As a young boy, while working behind-the-scenes in New York City's Chatham Theater, Ira Frederick Aldridge dreamed of becoming an actor. He was so successful in pursuit of this goal that he later became an international star. His dramatic interpretations of Shakespearean characters, particularly Othello, were so compelling that he won the admiration of people from all walks of life, including European audiences and royalty.

Ira was born in New York City, on or about July 24, 1807. His father was Daniel Aldridge, a straw vendor and preacher, and his mother, whose name is unknown, died when he was sixteen. Ira attended New York's African Free School, where he exhibited an early interest in the theater. His first performance was as Rolla in the New York African Theater's production of *Pizarro* by August von Kotzebue.

Sensing that greater theatrical opportunities were in Europe, in 1824, he worked his way across the ocean as a steward. He struck up a friendship with actors Henry and James Wallack, and he made the appropriate contacts. On October 10, 1825, he opened at the Royal Coburg in London in *The Revolt of Surinam, or A Slave's Revenge*. This debut was followed by many other top performances at the Royal Coburg, including *The Death of Christophe, King of Haiti*.

After fulfilling his commitments at the Royal Coburg, Aldridge appeared at the Theatre Royal in Brighton, England, where he portrayed Oroonoko and Othello. His interpretation of Othello was so authentic and moving that stage lore says the highly noticeable actress portraying Desdemona actually screamed out in genuine terror. It was this type of performance which won him the distinction of being one of the greatest actors of the time.

The high point of Aldridge's life came in 1833, when he appeared at the world-renowned Theatre Royal, Covent Garden in London, recreating his role of Othello. Again, his performance left audiences spellbound. Aldridge toured

Europe drawing from his repertoire to bring to the stage such characters as Mungo, Macbeth, Shylock, Lear, Richard III, and Othello. And, he revived the play, *Titus Andronicus*, winning critical acclaim as Aaron the Moor.

Aldridge was awarded many honors, including the Order of the Chevalier from the King of Prussia, and the Cross of Leopold from the Emperor of Austria. He personally performed before the King of Sweden. The rulers of Austria, Germany, and czarist Russia were treated to command performances. The Republic of Haiti saluted him as "the first man of colour in the theatre."

Aldridge was married to an Englishwoman and, after her death in 1864, he married Amanda Pauline von Brandt, with whom he had three children. In 1867, he was making plans to tour his native country of America after completing a tour in Lodz, Poland, however, a fatal lung infection caused his death on August 7, 1867.

Since his death, many distinctions have been bestowed upon the memory and accomplishments of Ira Aldridge. The Howard University's theater in Washington, D.C. is named in his honor. His name also is inscribed in the Shakespeare Memorial Theater at Stratford-upon-Avon in England. There, in the fourth row is a seat that bears the inscription of the man known as the greatest Shakespearean actor of his time, Ira Frederick Aldridge.

MARIAN ANDERSON
1903 - 1993

Known as the contralto of the century, Marian Anderson is one of the greatest singers of all time—Black or White. With her rich and moving voice, she captivated the world and made history on January 17, 1955, when she became the first Black to appear on the stage of the Metropolitan Opera House.

Marian Anderson was born in South Philadelphia, PA, on February 27, 1903. Her father sold coal and ice, and her mother was a domestic. She displayed an early talent for singing, and she supplemented her parent's meager income by singing at church concerts.

In high school, Marian's talent came to the attention of her teachers, who urged her to take voice lessons. Eventually, she auditioned for the famed voice tutor, Giuseppe Borghetti, who accepted her as his talented pupil. Her first-year tuition was paid from the nickels and dimes collected by her church members. Borghetti was so moved that he gave her the second year of lessons free.

In 1929, Marian won the Julius Rosenwald Scholarship and, like other Black artists, had to seek artistic refuge, fame and fortune in Europe. In 1933, desperate to make a concert appearance, she paid a concertmaster $500 to accompany her in Berlin. The audiences were entranced by her voice, which she flawlessly controlled in three octaves. With her repertoire of Bach, Beethoven and Negro spirituals, she brought audiences to their feet. She also awed her listeners with her ability to sing in nine different languages.

In 1938, Marian began a frantic concert pace, performing 92 recitals in 70 cities and logging 26,000 miles in a five-month span. She became one of the world's most popular and highest paid performers on the concert circuit. Although her talent rose above racism, in 1939, the Daughters of the American Revolution refused to allow her to perform in Washington, D.C.'s Constitution Hall. This snub ignited national outrage and resulted in Eleanor Roosevelt, wife of President Franklin D. Roosevelt, resigning her DAR membership.

Later, Anderson would write of the President's wife; "I suspect that she has done a great deal for people that has never been divulged publicly. I know what she did for me." Having become a cause celebre, Anderson was invited by Mrs. Roosevelt to perform at an outdoor concert on Easter Sunday, in 1939, at the Lincoln Memorial. An audience of 75,000 heard her perform one of her most successful recitals.

As evidence of her desire to help those who came after her, in December, 1945, she established the Marian Anderson Award to help advance careers of young, struggling singers. One of her lifelong desires was to perform at the Metropolitan Opera House, but no Black had ever achieved this feat. On January 17, 1955, however, she mounted the stage and made history with her outstanding performance. For this, and other achievements, she earned many awards.

In 1965, on Easter Sunday, Marian Anderson capped a triumphant career with her final concert at Carnegie Hall, in New York City. Following this, she retired with her husband, architect Orpheus H. Fisher, to their Danbury, Connecticut farm. At the age of 90, Marian Anderson died. However, her phenomenal talent as a contralto, the legion of fans she attracted from all over the world, and the racist barriers she overcame, made her a heroine to all aspiring for success against great odds.

JOSEPHINE BAKER
1906 -1975

Certainly one of the most colorful enter-tainers and controversial personalities of all time was dancer and singer Josephine Baker. Her temptress style and flair for the unusual made her a legend. Wearing her Blackness with a special pride, she pioneered by perform-ing in famous nightspots, thereby shat-tering that racial barrier.

Josephine Baker was born in St. Louis, on June 3, 1906, to Louis and Cary Baker. Josephine's mother raised her four children while working as a laundress. In school, Josephine fantasized about being an entertainer, but to augment the family income, she left school and started working as a domestic when she was eight years old. Her fantasy became reality when, at age 15, she joined a traveling dance show. Her success then led to engagements in the chorus of Noble Sissle's *Shuffle Along, Chocolate Dandies* on Broadway, and a stint at the Plantation Club.

While she was winning Black audiences, she failed to arouse the interests of the general population because she was Black. Therefore, when she was offered a major dancing role, for $250 a week, in *La Reve Negre,* which opened in the Theatre des Champs-Elysees in Paris, in October, 1925, she followed the path of many other Black performers by leaving for Europe. She played to standing-room-only audiences with such dances as the Black Bottom and Charleston, dances which were previously unknown in Paris.

Between 1928 and 1930, she took her show on the road and successfully toured 25 European cities. In 1930, she added singing to her act and made her formal debut as a singer-dancer at the Casino in Paris, where she received star billing. This was a prelude to her appearance in the *Follies Bergere,* where her name appeared in 20-foot neon lights. While in the *Follies,* she is said to have received 40,000 love letters and 2,000 offers of marriage.

Ever adventurous, Baker then tried her hand at movies and an operetta. In 1936, she returned to America and appeared in the *Ziegfeld Follies*. The reception was cool. In 1937, she returned to France and became a citizen, and was an admitted spy for the French Resistance Movement. For her loyalty, she earned the Legion of Honor and Rosette of the Resistance medals. In 1951, Baker, at age 44, returned to the Strand Theater in the United States, this time as an overwhelming success.

With a love for animals and for orphaned children, she purchased a 300-acre estate and chateau, known as *Les Milandes*, which she populated with animals of almost every breed and 14 children of every hue and nationality. Their variety prompted her to call them her "rainbow family." The children's nationalities were Korean, Columbian, Finnish, French, Japanese, Israeli, Arab, Venezuelan, and African.

Josephine Baker took personal stands against racism by refusing to play anywhere that barred Blacks as patrons. Her contract contained a non-discrimination clause; and legend has it that the famed Copa City Club in Miami changed its racial policy. As a result, all of Miami's clubs opened their doors to Blacks. Nearing 60 years of age, Baker participated in the March on Washington in August of 1963, and gave a benefit performance for civil rights in New York's Carnegie Hall, in October.

Josephine Baker, at age 69, died in Paris on April 12, 1975. However, she left a tradition of showmanship, a disposition toward charity, and a sense of Black pride. Josephine Baker was a legend in her own time.

JAMES BALDWIN
1924 -1987

James Baldwin ranks as one of the most prolific Black playwrights, essayists, and novelists of modern time. Throughout his works, he consistently treated racial discrimination as a disease of White society.

Born in New York City, August 2, 1924, to David and Berdis Emma Baldwin, James was the oldest of nine children. His father was a minister, so James was raised in a strict religious family. Following in his father's footsteps, he became a preacher when he was 14. Baldwin's genius surfaced as a student at DeWitt Clinton High School in New York, where he wrote the school's song, and was the editor of the school's magazine.

As his writing skill improved, Baldwin gave up preaching to follow his literary interests. After graduating from high school in 1942, and following the death of his father, Baldwin moved to Greenwich Village where he wrote for a variety of magazines. He also began what would eventually become his first novel. Meanwhile, he met the famed author of *Native Son*, Richard Wright; and largely through Wright's influence, Baldwin obtained the Eugene F. Saxton Memorial Trust Award in 1945, and the Rosenwald Fellowship in 1948.

Like other Black artists, Baldwin felt his creativity stifled by the White perception that he was just another "Negro writer." Therefore he left America for Paris, where he spent ten years. He was often lonely and sometimes very hungry, but the relative absence of racial prejudice gave him courage to write. In 1953, his first book, *Go Tell it On the Mountain*, partly autobiographical, was published. It was very successful, winning the praise of critics and launching a career that would see many of his stories and essays published worldwide in distinguished publications. For him, Paris was a haven of creativity. He associated with such noted authors as Norman Mailer and James Jones.

Following the success of his first book, Baldwin went on to write *Notes of a Native Son* (1955), a basically autobiographical account that analyzed Black-White relations. *Giovanni's Room* (1956), which was set in Paris, dealt with cruelty toward another minority, homosexuals. *Nobody Knows My Name*, published in 1961, was selected as one of the outstanding books of the year by the American Library Association. Other novels that followed were Another Country (1962); *Going to Meet the Man* (1965); *Tell Me How Long the Train's Been Gone* (1968); *A Rap on Race* (with Margaret Mead in 1971); *No Name in the Street* (1972), and *A Dialogue* (with Nikki Giovanni in 1972).

Baldwin also scored literary triumphs with his plays, *Blues for Mr. Charlie* (1964), which opened on Broadway, on April 23, 1964. By now, the movement for Black civil rights was in full swing, and Baldwin dedicated *Blues* to the memory of the victims of the South's racial violence. *The Amen Corner* (1965) also won critical acclaim. Some of the most fiery and significant essays of Black protest was Baldwin's *The Fire Next Time* and *Nobody Knows My Name : More Notes of a Native Son.*

For his literary triumphs, Baldwin received a host of honors, including a Guggenheim Literary Fellowship, a Ford Foundation grant-in-aid, a Partisan Review Fellowship, and a National Institute of Arts and Letters Award in 1956. In the later 1950s, Baldwin returned to Greenwich Village, where he continued to write, among other works, a television documentary on his childhood.

Baldwin died on December 1, 1987. Once, writing about himself, he mentioned his goal; "I want to be an honest man and a good writer." James Baldwin achieved his goal.

THOMAS GREEN BETHUNE
1849 -1908

Thomas Green Bethune, or "Blind Tom" as he was known on the concert circuit, has earned a lasting place in history for his musical genius. As a musical wonder, he astonished the international world with his compositions, memory, and keyboard tricks.

Thomas was born a slave on May 25, 1849, near Columbus, Georgia, the twentieth child of Charity Wiggins. Blind from birth, he was purchased by Colonel James Bethune in a deal that included both his parents. Even as an infant, he exhibited musical genius. When he was four, his master bought his daughters a piano. However, it was Tom who displayed eyebrow-raising skills on the piano.

Dubbed as the "musical marvel" on the Bethune plantation, even as early as age five, Tom could fluidly play Bach, Beethoven, Chopin, Liszt and Thalberg. He eventually had 5,000 songs in his repertoire. After hearing a song only once, he could play it perfectly, a demonstration of his retentive skills and his perfect pitch. He also composed more than 100 original compositions. That he achieved these feats with virtually no formal instruction only added to his reputation. However, he practiced as much as eight hours daily to keep his talent fine-tuned.

Tom's childlike behavior and penchant for making animal-like gestures, caused his mother to believe he was feeble-minded. Because her judgement of him was clouded by this belief, it was hard for her to understand his talent. However, recognizing Tom's marketability, Colonel Bethune persuaded Tom's parents to make him Tom's guardian. After this, he arranged a concert tour, where a larger audience testified to Tom's genius.

One of the tricks that left audiences spellbound was Bethune's ability to play compositions with his back to the piano. His musical wizardry was challenged by musical theorists, who presented him with tests of total recall. He passed the exams effortlessly and added these experts to his legion of fans. Bethune also played the coronet and wrote poetry. He became such a curiosity that, in 1860, he performed before President James Buchanan and a gathering of foreign dignitaries in Washington, D.C. It is believed that, "Blind Tom" earned over $100,000 for his master on the concert and vaudeville circuits.

Eventually, Colonel Bethune released his managerial and guardianship reins and turned Bethune over to his son, John G. Bethune. However, in 1883, the son died; and Bethune was taken over by John's widow, Eliza Bethune. In 1893, she married an attorney, Albert Lerche, and Tom's ownership was taken over by the couple. A legal tug-of-war ensued with the Lerches and the prodigy's first owner, Colonel Bethune. However, Colonel Bethune lost, and Tom's earnings were turned over to the Lerches.

Bethune's mother finally recognized the degree to which her son was being exploited and, unsuccessfully, fought to get him back. Despite having increased the net worth of others because of his talent, Blind Tom died penniless on June 13, 1908. He is remembered, however, not for his destitute ending, but for his bountiful talent, which has served as an inspiration for other entertainers who did not allow a handicap to stifle the development of their God-given talent.

R. NATHANIEL DETT
1882 - 1943

The elevation of Black spirituals from a folk music to the concert stage is credited to Robert Nathaniel Dett, one of the most prolific musical composers and choral leaders of all time. His special passion for Black spirituals inspired many of his compositions. While he cultivated and nurtured many Black choral groups, his talent attracted a multi-racial following.

Nathaniel Dett was born on October 11, 1882, in Ontario, Canada, to Charlotte and Robert Dett, who were well-educated and musically inclined. His grandmother, often sang Black spirituals, and it was from her that Dett gained a true appreciation for this music. Dett began playing the piano at age three, and had his first formal piano lesson at age five.

From 1901 to 1903, he attended the Oliver Willis Halsted Conservatory. In 1908, he received a bachelor's degree in music from Oberlin College. After being moved by the Kneisel Quartet singing a somber hymn, and the fond memories of his grandmother's songs, he turned his attention to elevating the Black spiritual to an art form. He carved his niche by composing a host of Black spirituals, including *Oh Holy Lord* and *Listen to the Lambs*, which continue to remain very popular and a staple for many Black spiritual choral groups.

In 1913, he began teaching at Hampton Institute, where he stayed until 1932 and where he made his biggest contribution. He founded the famed Musical Arts Society at Hampton Institute in 1919. He put Hampton Institute's choir on the international map by cultivating the talents of each member, merging them into a group talent, and taking them on international tours, where they delighted audiences the world over. He was a dedicated teacher, concerned about his students. He was also careful to present a good role model for them with his belief in scholastic achievement and hard work.

On December 27, 1916, he married Helen Elise Smith of New York City, an honor graduate of the Institute of Musical Arts in New York City and an accomplished concert pianist.

From this union, Helen and Josephine were born. In 1920, Dett took a leave from Hampton to attend Harvard University. There, he came to the attention of a wider music community, when he won the Bowdoin Prize for his essay, *The Emancipation of Negro Music.* He then received the Francis Boot Prize for the best vocal concert music composition, *Don't Be Weary Traveler.* He also earned honorary doctor of music degrees from Howard University in 1924, and from Oberlin in 1926. He received the Harmon Award for achievement in music, in 1927.

Dett also attended the American Conservatory of Music in Chicago, the Fountainebleau School of Music in France, and the Eastman School of Music in Rochester, New York. There, he earned a Master of Music degree in composition, in 1932, and there his thesis, *Composition for Chorus and Orchestra,* was later published as the opera, *The Ordering of Moses.* This opera was given national exposure by the National Negro Company at Carnegie Hall, in 1951.

In 1937, he began teaching at Bennett College in Greensboro, North Carolina, where he remained until 1942. In 1943, he joined the USO as a musical adviser, a post that sent him to Battle Creek, Michigan. It was while on this assignment that he died suddenly of a heart attack on October 2, 1943.

Nathaniel Dett lives in history as a man who brought another dimension to music, not only through his original compositions, but also through his ability to elevate the Black spiritual to a true musical art form.

CHARLES DEAN DIXON
1915 -1976

When he was 13, a teacher almost ended Charles Dean Dixon's career when she urged his mother to "stop wasting her money" and discontinue his musical studies. Fortunately, his mother ignored the advice. Her son went on to become the first Black to conduct a major symphony orchestra, and to achieve fame in many of the capitals of Europe.

Dean, as he was more popularly known, was born January 10, 1915, to West Indian parents. His mother, a music lover, who disliked popular music, took her young son frequently to Carnegie Hall to expose him to finer sounds. He also began taking violin lessons when he was three. His mother's persistence paid off, when he became so talented on the violin that he began playing the instrument while a student at DeWitt Clinton High School in Harlem.

Dixon also began to exhibit a great interest in becoming a conductor. Pursuing this interest, he organized the Dean Dixon Symphony in 1932; and with money gleaned from his own allowance, financed and nurtured the make-shift symphony into a 70-piece orchestra that entertained audiences in the neighborhood.

That same year, on the strength of a violin audition, Dixon was accepted into the Julliard Institute of Musical Art where he received his B.S. degree. Subsequently, he received a conductor's fellowship at the Julliard Graduate School, where he mastered all of the orchestra instruments under the watchful tutelage of the aimed Albert Stoessel. In 1938, he conducted the 38-piece League of Music Lovers Chamber Orchestra at a Town Hall concert. In 1939, he earned a master's degree from Columbia University Teachers College.

In 1941, Dixon returned to conducting at the urging of Eleanor Roosevelt, who had seen him conduct and give a concert at the Heckscher Theatre. Opportunity knocked because Samuel Chotzinoff, musical director of the National Broadcasting

Company symphony, was in the audience. He was so impressed with Dixon that he eventually made him the director of the NBC Symphony Orchestra. This was followed by conducting the New York Symphony Orchestra for two concerts, after which he was cheered by the orchestra members as well as the audience. A high moment in his career occurred in 1948, when he received the $1,000 Alice M. Ditson Award as the Outstanding Music Conductor of the Year.

Despite these moments of acclaim, Dixon wanted to be a permanent music conductor in America. However, racism limited his opportunities and, frustrated, he went to Europe in 1949, where he achieved the status that eluded him in America. He conducted orchestras all over the world. While he was in self-imposed exile, he introduced over 50 American works to the greater European audiences.

In 1960, Dixon was named conductor of the symphony orchestra in Frankfurt, Germany. In 1968, he returned to America where, during the Olympics in Mexico, he conducted the Mexican National Symphony Orchestra. During this historic event, he was billed as the "distinguished American conductor."

In 1970, over 20 years after he left America to achieve fame and fortune in a foreign land, Dixon was invited back to the United States, and he conducted orchestras for various concerts in American cities across the nation. Charles "Dean" Dixon died on November 3, 1976, but his sense of mission and will to succeed remain a beacon of hope to others who tread into frontiers not common for Black artists.

ALEXANDRE DUMAS
1802 - 1870

For years, adventure lovers have delighted in the exploits of Porthos, Aramis, and Athos, The Three Musketeers. Equally popular is the forerunner of all adventure novels, The Count of Monte Cristo. While these works are known romantic masterpieces, what is not widely known is that their author, Alexandre Dumas, was a Black man.

Alexandre Dumas was a mulatto whose father was Haitian born and whose mother was White. He was born Alexandre Davy de la Pailleterie, but abandoned that name when his father severed ties from Alexandre's grandfather and adopted his mother's maiden name, Dumas. Born in Villers-Cotterets in France, Dumas grew up in poverty but received an education from a local priest.

In 1827, Dumas traveled to Paris, the hub of literary activity, where he launched his career as a playwright. To support himself, he worked as a clerk. He then collaborated with a friend to write various vaudeville skits and, finally in 1829, he received critical acclaim for his play, *Henry III et Sa Cour*. This play was regarded as the first great triumph of romantic drama. Eventually, Dumas came to the attention of the Duke of Orleans and, with the Duke's backing, he churned out a phenomenal 40 plays in 15 years. Some of his more noteworthy efforts were *Anthony Richard Arlington* and *Mademoiselle de Belle-Isle*.

In 1839, Dumas entered upon another literary career, when he began writing historical romance novels. It was out of this new endeavor that *Three Musketeers* (eight volumes), *Twenty Years After* (ten volumes), and *The Count of Monte Cristo* (12 volumes) were published. His works were in such demand that he hired a corps of assistants to prepare outlines of stories. Dumas would convert these classics into the romantic novels that delighted his growing legion of admirers. His life, too, became a series of romantic adventures, which all of Paris tolerated because of his writing.

As added evidence of his literary ability, Dumas also published a newspaper, *Le Mousquetaire*, for four years. This, and other ventures, made him a wealthy man. With this money, he was able to erect his own theatre where, under his own artistic guidance, he produced his own plays. His flamboyant manner pleased his audiences as well as literary connoisseurs encountered on his world travels. In fact, among Parisians, he was reminiscent of a Hercules because of his "great height, his strong and squarely-built figure, his perpetually smiling face, his large head crowned with curly grey locks ... his deep chest and his firm step."

Dumas was certainly a giant in literature. Long after his death in 1870, he remains a literary hero who, despite the handicap of being a Black in a foreign land, forged an international reputation for himself. His own son, Alexandre Dumas, followed in his father's footsteps by becoming a famous author as well, enjoying even greater contemporary prestige than his father. Today, the son's reputation rests solely on his earliest play, *Camille*. It is Dumas senior's works that have achieved immortality.

ROBERT DUNCANSON
1817 - 1872

The most accomplished Black painter before the Civil War was Robert Duncanson, recognized before his death as "the best landscape painter in the West." Critics hailed him for his sensitivity to the beauty of landscape and "the very personal poetry" of his painting. He also was a muralist and portrait painter.

Robert Duncanson was born in New York in 1817, the son of a Scottish father and a mulatto mother. His mixed heritage plagued him, creating identity problems throughout his lifetime. At an early age, he was taken by his father to Canada to receive a formal education.

During Duncanson's formative teenage years, he showed a mastery for painting and, by age 20, he had attracted a devoted clientele. By this time, he was living in Ohio with his mother. The Freedmen's Aid Society of Ohio raised money to send him to Glasgow, Scotland, where he studied painting for three years.

Duncanson adopted the Huron River School of landscape painting and was greatly influenced by William L. Sonntag. He returned to Ohio in 1842, where his works went on display at various art museums in Cincinnati. Between 1845 and 1853, he traveled in New England, North Carolina, Pennsylvania and Michigan, where he created landscapes that depicted those beautiful areas.

In 1853, he returned once again to Europe, this time with Sonntag. Through a letter of introduction, he met the famed sculptor Hiram Powers, who may have had an influence on his work. Duncanson's paintings were displayed in Glasgow and other Scottish cities. He painted the famous *Trial of Shakespeare,* which was surpassed only by *Land of the Lotus Eaters,* another of his more celebrated renderings. He mingled easily with diverse cultural circles and attracted a legion of fans, including the Duchess of Sutherland, Alfred Lord Tennyson, and well-respected art critics.

Duncanson traveled to Europe again in 1863. It was rumored that this second visit abroad was prompted by a growing sense of resentment among Whites to the Civil War and Blacks in general. Nevertheless, his artistic ability was not smothered. In fact, as a result of his visits to Scotland and to many of the scenes depicted in Sir Walter Scott's novels, he painted some particularly noteworthy landscapes.

Duncanson returned to America in 1867, but his thirst for the stimulating life of Europe caused him to return to Scotland in 1870. However, it was said that persistent racial problems in America were again a motivating factor for his return to Europe. Throughout his life, Duncanson suffered from racial identity problems. He was snubbed by Whites, although his talent brought him to their attention. Because of this, he was dubbed "The Tragic Mulatto." Whether these factors contributed to his insanity or death is unknown, but records state that, on December 21, 1872, he died in Detroit.

Since his death, Duncanson's work has been exhibited at the Cincinnati Art Museum, where from March 16 to April 30, 1972, 35 of his paintings were displayed during a Centennial Exposition. History has judged him, according to one critic, "a conscientious artist working skillfully and imaginatively." The tragedy of his life was that society would not allow him to be comfortable in his own skin.

■ EDWARD KENNEDY "DUKE" ELLINGTON ■
1899 -1974

Called "the greatest single talent in the history of jazz," Edward Kennedy "Duke" Ellington was a musical impresario, whose 50 years in the entertainment business brought him fame and honor. He composed over 900 songs, many of which are American classics. And, the ongoing popularity of his music testifies to his talent, which made him one of the greatest entertainers of all time.

Duke Ellington was born on April 29, 1899, in Washington, D.C., to Daisy Kennedy Ellington and father, a draftsman, who worked nights as a butler to supplement the family income. In early years, Edward earned the nickname "Duke" because of his flair and style of dressing.

In high school, because Duke showed a talent for art, it didn't appear that he was destined for musical greatness. He was even offered an art scholarship to study at the Pratt Institute in New York. But, the lure of music was strong and, on a part time basis, he played with local bands. He had played the piano since age seven and, while working as a soda jerk in high school, he composed his first song, *Soda Fountain Rag.*

In 1918, he formed his own band, Duke's Serenaders, which performed for local social gatherings. In 1927, his band was contracted to perform at Harlem's famed Cotton Club and it became the top attraction. In 1933, the band toured Europe, where he became known internationally. For the remainder of his life, he and his band entertained worldwide audiences in the vaudeville circuit, Broadway, musical revues, motion pictures, recordings, and at standing-room-only concerts.

During this time, Ellington also composed songs, which displayed his musical versatility. His classics include *Mood Indigo* and *Don't Get Around Much Anymore.* Other Duke Ellington compositions were *Solitude, Sophisticated Lady, Caravan,* and the classic *Take the A Train. Mood Indigo* was written in 15 minutes, while he was waiting for his mother to finish dinner. In 1943, Duke tried his hand at a new musical form when he wrote the *Black, Brown and Beige Suite*, which captured, in a choral poem, the joys and travails of being Black. His musical tribute to Black people, *My People*, also won critical acclaim.

While his entire life was marked by high points, there were particular climatic moments in his life. In June, 1965, for example, he and his orchestra played his *Far East Suite* at the White House Festival of the Arts. One month later, the New York Philharmonic Orchestra brought his new score to life, *The Golden Broom and the Golden Apple*, at New York's Lincoln Center.

Duke Ellington was recommended for a Pulitzer Prize for his special contribution to music in 1965, but the nomination was denied. Nevertheless, he continued making musical history. On his 70th birthday, on April 29, 1969, he was the guest of honor at a White House dinner hosted by President Richard Nixon, who awarded him the Presidential Medal of Freedom, the highest award bestowed upon a civilian.

At the age of 75, on May 24, 1974, Duke Ellington died. The nation's King of Swing was gone, but his legacy lives on with his son, Mercer, who continues his musical tradition. It also lives on in the thousands of musical notes he wrote and the lingering pleasure they continue to give.

META VAUX WARRICK FULLER
1877 - 1968

Rodin and St. Gaudens, two of the world's most famous sculptors, were mentors for Meta Vaux Warrick Fuller, who became a celebrated sculptress herself. Over a 70-year span, she faced racial discrimination and misfortune, emerging triumphant and successful.

Meta's journey into history began on June 9, 1877, when she was born to William and Emma Jones Warrick. From an early age, Meta showed a talent for the performing arts, but it was when she was singled out for special art lessons that the talent became dominant. In 1894, she received a three-year scholarship to study her craft at the Liberty Tadd's Industrial Art School, at the Pennsylvania Museum of Fine Arts. In 1898, the year was highlighted by her winning a prize for her metalwork piece, *Crucifixion of Christ in Agony*. The next year, she went to Paris to further refine her talent.

While Fuller cultivated her talent at various Paris art academies, her first two years were marked by financial difficulties. Meta explored bolder art subjects and gave a series of showings at Paris galleries, where her works were a favorite of art buyers. After a triumphant and lucrative final year in Paris, Meta returned to Philadelphia only to find a lack of interest in her work.

In 1907, however, Meta was commissioned to sculpt 150 Black figures for the Jamestown Tercentennial Exposition, marking the landing of English settlers at Jamestown in 1607. Her work depicted the progress of Blacks since that period and, for graphically bringing this progression to life, she won a gold medal.

Two years later, on February 3, 1909, she married Dr. Solomon C. Fuller, a native of Liberia and a neurologist. The couple moved to Framingham, Massachusetts, where, eventually, they had three sons. In 1910, a fire at a warehouse, where her works were stored destroyed virtually all of her pieces of art. Her interest in art was temporarily abandoned, and she concentrated on raising her three sons for the next few years. The artistic spark was re-ignited in 1913, when W.E.B. DuBois asked her to create a piece that symbolized the spirit of the 50th anniversary celebration of the *Emancipation Proclamation*. The result was a statue that showed a black boy and girl, which marked the real beginning of her use of Blacks as subjects. The next 50 years saw her works in demand at churches, libraries, art clubs, galleries, and from a growing consumer audience.

From 1950 to 1955, her husband's illness and subsequent death, and her own bout with tuberculosis forced her to take a break from her work. After overcoming this string of adversities, Fuller returned to sculpting and found that her talent was at its peak, when she was commissioned by a group of organizations to create sculptures for them. In a gala celebration sponsored by Howard University in March, 1961, she was recognized as one of three outstanding sculptors. One of her last pieces, *The Crucifixion*, with the head of Christ raised, was a tribute to the four little Black girls killed, in 1963, during a church bombing in Birmingham, Alabama.

On March 13, 1968, Meta Fuller died of natural causes. Today, her works can be seen in such prestigious places as the Arthur Schomburg collection in the New York Public Library, the Boston Museum of Afro-American History, and the Cleveland Museum of Art. Meta Vaux Warrick Fuller is recognized as a gifted and celebrated sculptor of international importance.

WILLIAM CHRISTOPHER (W.C.) HANDY
1873 -1958

W.C. Handy has earned his rightful place in musical history as the "Father of the Blues." He popularized the folk music that had been sung for years by generations of southern Blacks, and gave it to the rest of the world.

Handy was born in a log cabin in Florence, Alabama, on November 16, 1873, the grandson of slaves. His father and grandfather before him were both ministers, so in William, they saw someone who would carry on their work in the pulpit. However, from the beginning, Handy was drawn to music.

In 1893, after attending the Florence District School, where he studied music, he formed his own quartet and also barnstormed the country with various brass bands playing the cornet, primarily, at minstrel shows. Eventually, he formed his own band, the Mahara Minstrels Troup, and they traveled the United States, Cuba, and Mexico, playing marches and Stephen Foster's tunes. Meanwhile, in 1898, he married his childhood sweetheart, Elizabeth V. Prince, with whom he had six children.

Largely due to his parent's influence, Handy harbored a disdain for the blues. He, like others, dismissed them as "lowlife" and substandard. However, during his travels in the rural south, he happened upon a band of poor musicians twanging a homemade guitar and singing the blues. This time, the music evoked a response from him. Instead of viewing the music with contempt, he saw a certain beauty in the tunes. He became so enchanted by that moment that he began devoting himself solely to the blues. Handy began composing blues tunes with a frenzy. He remained consistent in his style, adopting a 12-bar structure and plaintive lyrics that told the trials and tribulations of being a Black person in the South.

A chance event catapulted Handy into fame in 1909. That was the year Memphis "Boss" Edward H. Crump hired him to write a song that would promote Crump's mayoral campaign. The song, a mixture of ragtime and blues, was initially known as *Mr. Crump*. The tune was so catchy, it became popular. After the election, he renamed it *Memphis Blues*, and it was the beginning of real success. He teamed up with Harry Pace to launch the Pace and Handy Music Company, a music-publishing concern.

Under the banner of his company, in 1914, Handy composed the *St. Louis Blues*, and retained the musical rights to this tune. In his lifetime, he earned over $1 million in royalties from this song alone. Other popular tunes authored by Handy, included *Aunt Hagar's Blues; A Good Man is Hard to Find; and Careless Love*. By this time, he had attracted a huge White audience, whose support solidified his success.

In 1937, tragedy entered his life when his wife died. And, he was permanently blinded, in 1943, when he fell from a subway station. Undaunted, he continued publishing songs and working in his prosperous business. In 1954, he married Irma Louis Logan. One year later, he suffered a stroke that further impaired his health. Nevertheless, on November 17, 1957, he was the guest of honor at a party that was attended by over 800 celebrities and fans.

On March 28, 1958, W.C. Handy died at the Sydenham Hospital, in Harlem, New York, of acute bronchial pneumonia, thus ending an illustrious career. As a tribute to his greatness, a host of schools, parks, and theaters are named in his honor. The "Father of the Blues" aptly describes W.C. Handy and his musical contribution to the world.

LORRAINE VIVIAN HANSBERRY
1930 -1965

In her short life of only 35 years, Lorraine Hansberry made a vivid imprint on the American theater scene. In her first effort as a playwright, she authored A Raisin in the Sun, a masterpiece that captured the New York Drama Critics Circle Award as best play of the 1958-1959 season. It was the first time that a Black author had earned such a prize.

Lorraine was born in Chicago on May 19, 1930. Her father was a prosperous entrepreneur, who, like his wife Nannie, had migrated from the South to Chicago to find a more lucrative life. He became a successful realtor and banker. But when he purchased a home in an all-white neighborhood, racists, backed by Illinois law, protested, and the family was forced to move. However, he took the case to the Supreme Court and won, but the ordeal took a financial and psychological toll. In 1945, when he died of a cerebral hemorrhage, his plans to become a resident of Mexico ended. This experience greatly influenced Hansberry because, in her celebrated play, she would replay many of these events.

Hansberry attended Chicago public schools and was an avid reader. Several of her favorite writers were Langston Hughes, Countee Cullen, and historian Carter G. Woodson. Hansberry entered the University of Wisconsin, where she studied stage design and art, and discovered a love for the theater. In 1950, she went to New York, the heart of America's theater activity.

In 1951, while working as a waitress in a Greenwich Village restaurant, Lorraine met the owner's son, Robert Nemiroff. The pair were married and, with his support, she busied herself writing short stories, poetry, and plays. Between 1956 and 1957, she devoted all of her creative energies to writing *A Raisin in the Sun*. The plot centered on a Black Southside Chicago family striving to overcome their conflicts in the midst of a racist society.

On March 11, 1959, *A Raisin in the Sun* opened at Broadway's Ethel Barrymore Theater. Drama critics were ecstatic, and success was immediate. The play, which remains a classic, enjoyed a 19-month run, winning for its author the coveted Drama Circle Award. It was later adapted into a movie. The play thrust her into the limelight, and her public speaking and social appearances increased dramatically.

In 1963, cancer struck, and until Hansberry's death in 1965, she was frequently in the hospital. Resolved to continue writing, she completed her second Broadway play, *The Sign in Sidney Brustein's Window*, which opened October, 1964. On January 12, 1965, three months after the play opened, Hansberry died.

Hansberry's husband, as a tribute to her, compiled and edited *To Be Young, Gifted and Black*, which was published in 1969 and contains a compilation of autobiographical statements from her. It contains such wisdom as this: "Out of the depths of pain we have thought to be our sole heritage in this world. Oh, we know about love! Perhaps we shall be the teachers when it is done. And that is why I say to you that, though it be a thrilling and marvelous thing to be merely young and gifted in such times, it is doubly so, doubly dynamic, to be young, gifted, and Black."

Lorraine Hansberry's full potential will never be known because her life was shortened. But, as a Black Broadway playwright, she was preceded by very few, and none of them women.

When it comes to the love of guitar playing, Justin Holland was about 150 years ahead of his time. He was a virtuoso guitar player, whose books remain the favorite instructional texts for mastering this instrument.

Justin was born in Norfolk County, Virginia, in 1819, to Exum Holland, a farmer. Even as a child, he had such an attraction to music that he walked ten miles every Sunday to participate in a songfest.

When he was 14, he moved to Boston. While attending a local concert, he heard a Spanish guitarist named Marian Perez. He was passionately moved, not only by the guitarist and his talent, but also by the acoustics produced by the sound. Of this experience, he wrote, "I ... thus discovered the true theory of the harmonic tones to be the vibrations of a single string in a number of equal sections, more or less, and all at the same time; and that their production was at his pleasure of the operator as he desired higher or lower tones."

He resolved to emulate his newly-found idol. He also studied under two instructors and added the mastery of the flute and piano to his repertoire of instruments. When he was 22, he enrolled in Oberlin College to continue his studies.

At age 26, Holland moved to Cleveland, where he became successful as a guitar teacher, musical scholar, and arranger. Until his arrival on the music scene, a guitar was merely a stepchild of other instruments. However, Holland devoted considerable time to adapting music for other instruments to the guitar. By 1848, through a successful marketing campaign, he published and sold these arrangements with considerable success. With guitar arrangements now in greater distribution, this instrument gained a wider appeal and acceptance.

In 1874, Holland wrote *Holland's Comprehensive Method for the Guitar*. In 1876, a revised edition, *Holland's Modern*

Method for the Guitar, became the standard text for guitar playing. Widely sold, these texts represented Holland's greatest contribution to music.

Holland preferred to devote his time to teaching and writing rather than as a paid performer. Although most of his students were White, he refrained from letting social issues of the day interfere with his teacher/student relationship. With mutual respect extended, he kept his teaching on a strict business level. Always seeking to keep abreast of the latest musical developments worldwide, he mastered French, Italian, and Spanish.

Holland moved to New Orleans, where he passed away on March 24, 1886. While viewed in life as a musician whose genius raised him above others, his death also brought a series of tributes. The *Cleveland Plain Dealer* noted, "He stood foremost among the members of his profession ... His name is more widely known than any other American guitarist ... As a man, when one came to know him, the old professor possessed a heart flowing over with love for his pupils, and no favor was too great to be asked."

Most appropriate is a sentiment that captures the essence of Justin Holland's life; "He will be sadly missed in musical circles ... and it will be many years before Cleveland possesses another guitarist so gifted, so educated and so able to arouse a love for one of the noblest musical instruments."

LANGSTON HUGHES
1902 -1967

The entire literary spectrum, from po-ems to novels, was mastered by Lang-ston Hughes. But, he is remembered mainly as a leading poet of his race, "the Poet Laureate of Harlem." The com-mon man, his joys, pleasures, and sor-rows were recurring themes in most of Hughes' works.

Hughes was born February 1, 1902, in Joplin, Missouri, to James and Carrie Mercer (Langston) Hughes. In 1914, in Lincoln, Illinois, his budding writing talent emerged while in elementary and later high school. He then briefly attended Columbia University in New York City. It proved to be a banner year in 1921, when Hughes published his classic poem, *The Negro Speaks of Rivers in The Crisis.* He also showed his talent for drama with his sketch, *The Gold Piece,* which appeared in *The Brownies Book.*

In 1924, after spending two years in Europe, Hughes returned to the United States and worked as a bus boy in a Washington, D.C., restaurant frequented by poet Vachel Lindsay. One day, Hughes mustered up his courage and slipped Lindsay one of his poems. Lindsay was impressed with Hughes' poetic style of rhythm and, with Lindsay's support, Hughes published his first volume of poems, *The Weary Blues,* in 1926.

Also, in 1926, Hughes enrolled in Lincoln University in Pennsylvania, where he graduated in 1929. In 1927, while in college, his second volume of poetry was overwhelmingly successful. In 1930, he published his first novel, *Not Without Laughter,* which earned him the Harmon Award for Literature. This success generated several years of travel which included a poetry reading tour of the U.S., a trip to Haiti and the Soviet Union.

In 1937, after a time in Spain reporting on the Spanish Civil War, he returned to the United States and established theater groups in Harlem, Los Angeles, and Chicago. The year

1943 was a watershed year for this established creative genius. He introduced the character "Simple" in a column he authored for the Chicago Defender. He drew from his Harlem experiences in writing about Simple and his escapades and, as Simple, commented on social issues in a humorous vein.

Inspired by the Simple column, Langston wrote the novels, *Simple Speaks His Mind* (1950), *Simple Takes a Wife* (1953), *Simple Stakes a Claim* (1957), and *Simple's Uncle Sam* (1965). His other novels included *Tambourines to Glory* (1958). He also wrote an anthology of short stories including *The Ways of White Folks* (1934), *Laughing to Keep From Crying* (1952), and *Something in Common and Other Stories* (1963).

Hughes went on to prove himself the most versatile writer to come out of the Harlem Renaissance by writing a series of plays, most notably, *Little Ham* (1935), which is described as his most popular; the full-length musical drama, *Simply Heavenly;* the two-act comedy/musical, *Tambourines to Glory* (1963), and the gospel singing two-act play, *Soul Gone Home.* His notable poems include *The Dream Keeper* and *Ask Your Mama.* His biographies included *Famous American Negroes, Famous Negro Heroes,* and *Famous Negro Music Makers.*

Hughes also wrote books for children, musical lyrics, and traveled the country lecturing at schools and colleges. He received numerous honors for his works, and the fellowships awarded him made him even more famous. However, Langston Hughes died, a bachelor, on May 22, 1967, of congestive heart failure in New York City. His mission as a Black writer, stretched far beyond America's borders and earned for Hughes another title, "the most translated poet."

■ MATILDA SISSIERETTA JOYNER JONES ■
1869 -1933

Known more popularly as "Black Patti," Matilda Sissieretta Joyner Jones was so musically gifted that, had she been White, she would have been singing in the Metropolitan Opera House. Not until 1955 did the first Black, Marian Anderson, sing at the Met.

Matilda was born on January 5, 1869, in Portsmouth, Virginia, to a minister father, Rev. Jeremiah Malachi Joyner, and her mother, Henrietta B. Joyner, who was said to have had a rich soprano voice. When Matilda was only eight, the family moved to Providence, Rhode Island. When she was barely into her teens, she began formal training in music, at the Providence Academy of Music, under the tutelage of Ada, Baroness Lacombe.

Matilda reportedly studied voice under a private instructor at the New England Conservatory of Music. On September 4, 1883, she married David Richard Jones. In 1888, she launched her professional career with a performance in New York City. This was followed by a six-month tour of the West Indies with the Tennessee Jubilee Singers, a tour that earned her considerable praise from critics.

She gained particular acclaim in 1892, when she appeared at a Grand African Jubilee held in Madison Square Garden. A critic soon named her "Black Patti," after the Italian prima donna Adelina Patti. At first, Sissieretta Jones bristled at the name and the comparison it made. However, the name stuck, and she soon became so accustomed to it that she incorporated it into her act. Her successful performances prompted the managers of the Metropolitan Opera House to seriously consider booking her to play the dark roles in the productions of Aida and L'Africaine. However, racial prejudice prevented the consideration from becoming a reality.

"Black Patti" continued on the concert circuit and fulfilled other requests, including the invitation from President Harrison. She also sang at the Pittsburgh Exposition and then launched a yearlong concert tour that was said to have included a command performance for the Prince of Wales.

When Sissieretta Jones returned to America, she performed in the 1893 production, *Oriental America*, which featured an entirely Black cast. In 1899, she parlayed her popularity and versatile singing ability into her own variety show, *Black Patti's Troubadours*. The production featured a montage of entertainment, including a minstrel show, acrobatics, dancing, singing and vaudeville that was climaxed with Jones singing selections from operas.

The *Oriental America* traveling production played before audiences, Black and White, throughout the United States, Mexico, Cuba, the West Indies, and South America for 17 years. "Black Patti" earned the acclaim of a host of critics, and William Lictenwanger, the noted musicologist, observed that she "forced the musical and theatrical worlds in the United States to accept the Negro in a new image."

After the *Troubadours'* production ran its course, Jones retired, in 1916, to her home in Providence. Matilda Sissieretta Joyner Jones died of cancer on June 24, 1933. In life, she brought a special flair to the entertainment industry, and she cracked the door that would soon open to talented Blacks who came after her. She left an entertainment legacy that served as a guidepost and inspiration for future musical stars, which included Marian Anderson, Roland Hayes, and many others.

Scott Joplin is credited with founding and popularizing ragtime music, which was the forerunner to jazz. He also was the first American musician to compose American folk operas and ballads. Amazingly, Joplin achieved these major accomplishments without the benefit of formal training.

Joplin was born in 1868, in Texarkana, Texas, to a railroad laborer and his musically talented wife. He launched his professional piano-playing career as a teenager in 1884. Black boys had few opportunities in East Texas, except on the railroad or in the saw mills. Joplin saw music as a way of escape. In 1885, he moved to St. Louis, Missouri. He got a job playing piano in the Silver Dollar, a saloon owned by a true rag music lover, "Honest" John Turpin.

In 1895, Joplin moved to Sedalia, Missouri, where he began publishing songs and setting the stage for future success. In 1898, he composed his first rag compositions; *Original Rags* and *Maple Leaf Rag*, which was later published by John Stark and became a huge commercial success. The piece sold over one million copies and remains a rag music mainstay today. This success was followed by a series of other Joplin rag pieces, including *The Entertainer, Euphonic Sounds, Magnetic Rag* and *Wall Street Rag*. He also attended George Smith College for Negroes, where he studied theory and composition.

Joplin took his musical skills to still another level when, in 1899, he completed the folk ballad, *The Ragtime Dance*, which was performed in Sedalia's Woods Opera House. In 1900, he married Belle Hayden, who did not share Joplin's passion for music, and the marriage failed. He again entered into unexplored musical territory when, in 1903, he composed, *A Guest of Honor*, a rag opera which was performed by a group billed as the Scott Joplin Drama Company.

In 1905, Joplin completed his most ambitious musical undertaking when he wrote the opera, *Treemonisha*. It was composed of 27 numbers that covered the music spectrum from folksongs, spirituals and blues, and followed an opera format with an overture, prelude, recitatives, arias, small ensembles, choruses, and ballet. *Treemonisha* advanced the theme that education was the salvation of the Black race. This opera was an astonishing achievement for someone with no formal training in opera composition.

Joplin was not able to attract an audience for *Treemonisha*, so after moving to New York in 1907, he went back to more familiar musical grounds by managing a music studio and by composing new rags, including *Frog Legs Rag* and *Kansas City Rag*. In 1908, he also provided invaluable service to musical education by publishing a manual, *The School of Ragtime - Six Exercises for Piano*, in which he outlined the rudiments of mastering rag music. He also founded a publishing company and toured on the vaudeville circuit. In 1909, he married Lottie Stokes, who became one of his most ardent supporters.

Despite this success and personal happiness, Joplin was haunted by his opera, *Treemonisha*, and was so obsessed with getting it produced that he devoted considerable time and money to this effort. In 1911, he published the 230-page opera; and four years later, after unsuccessfully attempting to find a producer, he produced it himself in a Harlem hall. It was a total failure.

Joplin moved to Kansas City, Missouri, where until his death in 1917, he continued his various musical pursuits. In 1974, his classic, *The Entertainer*, was revived in the award-winning movie "The Sting." In so doing, Scott Joplin's name was introduced to an entirely new generation of admirers.

A forerunner of the modern day entertainer, who uses body and facial expressions to complement a performance, was a child prodigy named Florence Mills. A singer and dancer whose trademarks were strutting, stalking, cakewalking, and a pantomime style of mouthing, she won stardom in the United States and the world with her unique performance.

Florence was born to John and Nellie Simon Winfrey in 1895, in Washington, D.C. When she was only four years old, she made her debut as a professional performer in Williams' and Walker's *Sons of Ham,* where she brought the house down with her rendition of the song, *Hannah from Savannah.* By age six, she had so perfected her act that she was billed as "Baby Florence Mills," with a particular talent for the cakewalk and buck-dancing. Within two years, she became an accomplished performer.

When Florence was 15, she teamed up with her two older sisters, Olivia and Maude, to form the Mills Trio, which performed in vaudeville. Later, she broke away from her sisters and starred with Cora Green and Ada "Bricktop" Smith in the Panama Trio.

For the next decade, Mills crisscrossed the country performing on the vaudeville circuit. Her salary increased as she improved her act. Her big break came in September, 1921, when Gertrude Samuels, one of the leads in the Black revue, *Shuffle Along,* fell ill. Mills was chosen as the replacement, and her performance brought her stardom. Her bird-like singing tone captivated her audience. One of her most memorable performances was when, in her small voice, she sang her favorite song, *I'm a Little Blackbird Looking for a Bluebird.* Critics noted her ability to give her audiences lumps in their throats and tears in their eyes.

James Weldon Johnson praised Mills' talents by stating that "as a pantomimist and a singing and dancing comedienne, she had no superior in any place or any race." She also paved the way for future Blacks in the entertainment industry. Her show-stopping performances proved that Blacks could star in a musical show of high quality, which also could be an artistic and financial success. Critic Leslie Walton said "Her shows measured up to the high standards set with respect to class, cleanliness, and merit."

Shuffle Along was only the beginning of a long string of productions that saw Mills star in *Plantation Revue* (1922) at the New York Plantation Club; *from Dover to Dixie,* in London (1923), *Dixie to Broadway,* on Broadway in 1924, and *Blackbirds of 1926.* After *Blackbirds'* six-week Harlem run, it was performed in London for six months, where the Prince of Wales is said to have seen it 16 times. On October 12, 1927, she rushed back to New York for an urgent appendectomy. She died in the hospital, on November 1, of complications. She was only 32.

Florence Mills funeral attracted over 100,000 mourners. And, symbolically, when the hearse approached 145th Street in Harlem, an airplane released a flock of blackbirds, the ultimate salute to a rare jewel of talent, who left a permanent mark.

ALEXANDER SERGEYEVICH PUSHKIN
1799 - 1837

Alexander Sergeyevich Pushkin, great grandson of an African slave, became Russia's greatest poet. Greatness was a trait that ran in his family. His grandfather, Abraham Hannibal, an African who became a special favorite of Peter the Great, achieved fame in the armies of the Czars and as a renowned engineer. Pushkin's father was also a highly regarded engineer.

When Alexander was born on May 26, 1799, to Nedezhda and Ivan Pushkin, expectations were high that he would leave some significant imprint on the world. Very early, he enjoyed reading and displayed a talent for writing poetry. In 1811, he was sent to Tsarkoe Selo, near St. Petersburg, a school for aristocrats, where his writing skills were strengthened. Not only was he impressive because of his writing skills, but also because of his imposing African features.

In 1818, after he left the school, he was appointed to the ministry of foreign affairs. He worked for the government by day, and then enjoyed himself by writing poetry in the evening. His poems eventually were greatly admired in Russia's literary circles, and he was often called upon to recite them. As his fame increased, he came to be called "the greatest poet in all of Russia."

Around this same time, Russia became embroiled in a civil war; and Pushkin, through his poems, was critical of the Czarist regime of Alexander I. As a means of protest, he wrote, *Ode to Freedom*, and *Noel*. These poems quickly came to the attention of the government, and he was banished to the south of Russia to Ekaterinoslav. While in exile, he authored the six-part fairy tale in verse, *Ruslan and Ludmila*, one of his greatest poetic triumphs.

For nearly six years, Pushkin was transferred to different remote areas in Russia, where he continued to write. During this period, he wrote *Eugene Onegin,* which was inspired by the style of the English poet, Lord Byron, and *Bakchisarai*

Fountain. He began to earn his living as a poet, the first Russian ever to do so.

In 1824, he was discharged from government service and returned to his mother's village. Alexander I pardoned him on the condition that he would not provoke unrest through his future poems. Pushkin agreed. Among his new works were *Boris Godunov, Ode to Napoleon,* and *The Gypsies.* And while he agreed to avoid writing on issues concerning government, in his poem, *The Bronze Horseman,* he exhibited concern about the rights of the individual versus the state.

Pushkin also wrote two novels, *The Captive of the Caucasus* and *The Captain's Daughter,* one of his most memorable works. A running theme through his works was his obvious pride in his African roots. And, as a way of paying homage to his ancestors, he started the novel, *The Moor of Peter the Great,* an unfinished salute to his grandfather, Abram Hannibal.

He eventually married Nathaliee Goncharova, who is dismissed by historians as "beautiful but frivolous." Her cousin challenged Pushkin to a duel over her, and Pushkin was shot to death, thereby ending an illustrious career when he was only 38.

As a memorial to this great Russian poet, who ranks with Tolstoy and Dostoevski as Russian literary heroes, the country erected a statue, named a city and a theater in his honor. Alexander Sergeyvich Pushkin elevated writing to a profession in Russia. By doing so, he influenced virtually every writer who came after him.

PAUL ROBESON
1898 -1976

In almost everything he tried, Paul Robeson was an amazing success. As a boy, he was an outstanding scholar and athlete. Of the many careers he might have followed, he chose singing and acting.

Paul was born in Princeton, New Jersey, on April 9, 1898, to Anna Robeson, who was part Indian, and William Drew Robeson, a former slave who worked his way through Lincoln University and became a minister.

Paul Robeson attended Rutgers College on a scholarship. There, he won letters in many sports, and was an All-American in 1917 and 1918. He sang in the glee club, was a debating champion, and was elected Phi Beta Kappa. Robeson completed college and enrolled at Columbia University, where he earned his law degree. To support himself, he played professional football. Soon after graduating from Columbia, he went to work in a New York-based law firm.

In 1921, he married Eslanda Goode, and the union produced one son, Paul Jr. At his wife's urging, Robeson tried his hand at acting. Eventually, he appeared in *Emperor Jones* in New York and London; and it was during this production that his talent as a singer became evident. Particularly astonishing was the fact that he'd never had one singing lesson. Motivated by this success, he resigned from the law firm to devote his full time to the theater.

In the next two decades, Robeson became a star of stage, movies, radio and records. His acting credits included *All God's Chillun Got Wings,* and *Othello* at London's Savoy Theatre. This latter performance was so brilliant that critics from the *London Morning Post* raved that "there has been no 'Othello' on our stage, certainly for 40 years, to compare with his dignity, simplicity and true passion." Robeson also appeared in the early movie productions of *Emperor Jones,* *Showboat, Jericho, King Solomon's Mines,* and *Saunders of the River*

Robeson spoke Chinese and Russian fluently, and was competent in six other languages. Consequently, he was able to reach a wide audience in the more than 300 recordings he made. His acting ability was paralleled by his singing success. He sang folk songs and Negro spirituals with passion. His rendition of *Ol' Man River* was particularly moving. He was in such demand that concert tours took him to many cities in the United States and Europe.

Robeson made numerous trips to the Soviet Union, where he criticized the United States, particularly, for its treatment of Blacks. This ruined his career in the U.S. and, during the 1950s, he appeared before the House Committe on Un-American Activities and was targeted as a "Communist sympathizer." Robeson, however, stuck to his convictions and sent his only son to Russia to be educated. And, in 1952, he accepted the Stalin Peace Prize from the Soviet Union. In 1958, he and his family moved to Europe for a five-year exile, returning to the U.S. in 1963.

Robeson died January 23, 1976. In his senior years, the outrage that marked Robeson's younger days was replaced by his hope that the Black would eventually become "a full American in every sense of the word." Robeson's interest in Communism came at a time when America was paranoid on the subject. And while it shortened his career, it did not dim the memory of his exceptional talent.

LUTHER ROBINSON
(BILL "BOJANGLES")
1878 -1949

Among the classic scenes from American motion pictures is the one in The Little Colonel where child-star Shirley Temple dances up the magic staircase. The dancing teacher in this memorable movie was Luther (Bill "Bojangles") Robinson, perhaps the greatest tap dancer of all time.

Robinson was born in Richmond, Virginia, on May 25, 1878, the son of Maxwell Robinson, a machine-shop worker, and Maria Robinson, who had a talent for singing. Orphaned as a baby, he was reared by his grandmother. Against her wishes, he quit school when he was eight and ran away to Washington, D.C.

It was in Washington, D.C. that Robinson was first exposed to, and entranced by minstrel groups. He studied their popular dancing style and took the best aspects of their routines and incorporated them into his highly-spirited, rhythmic, complex and unique dancing style. By this time, he had adopted the name Bill after his brother William. Along the way, he also obtained the name "Bojangles," the origin from which is unknown, but immortalized in the song *Mr. Bojangles.*

In 1892, he joined a professional minstrel show, *The South Before the War,* which opened in New York City, and for which he was paid 50 cents per night. When the show ended, his career seemed over, too. For 10 years, he worked as a waiter back in Richmond.

In Chicago, in 1908, he met Marty Forkins and the pair struck up a lifelong alliance that saw Forkins become his manager and tutor. Robinson began perfecting his routine and he was rewarded by becoming a lead performer on the vaudeville circuit. He appeared in two major revues, *Blackbirds* (1928) and *Brown Buddies* (1933). By this time, he was a larger-than-life performer and had earned the nickname

"Dark Cloud of Joy," and the title, "The King of Tap Dancers." During this time, he also married Fannie S. Clay.

The period from 1929 to 1943 saw him performing in a series of motion pictures with Shirley Temple. One of the most notable was *The Little Colonel* (1935). Other movies were *The Little Rebel* (1935), *Rebecca of Sunnybrook Farm* (1938), and *Just Around the Corner* (1938), all with Shirley Temple.

Robinson left Hollywood once to appear in *Hot Mikado* (1939), a jazz version of the Gilbert and Sullivan operetta for which he won critical acclaim. His next Broadway performance was in *All in Fun* (1940), and his last was as a romantic lead to Lena Horne in the all-Black musical, *Stormy Weather* (1943). Also, in 1943, he and Fannie Clay were divorced and, in 1944, he married Elaine Plaines.

Robinson was a great ham as well as performer. He could run backwards faster than most people could run forward, and, on his 60th birthday, he displayed his stamina and showmanship by tap dancing up Broadway from 42nd Street to 110th Street. Also a humanitarian, Robinson made a habit of taking time out every year to lecture to the graduating class of Harlem's Public School 119. He would urge the students to "go high as you can."

Robinson died in 1949, at the age of 71. Over one million people paid their last respects, lining the streets of New York as the funeral procession went by. Many entertainers have tried to imitate him, but he was one of a kind. His talent took him from a salary of $5 a week to $6,500 a night. It also endeared him to a generation of Americans, who made him their folk hero.

Gimme a Pigfoot (... and a bottle of beer) was a song made on the last recording date of a woman known as "Queen of the Blues" and "Empress of the Blues." She was Bessie Smith, who sang her way into music history as one of the greatest entertainers and blues impresarios.

Bessie was one of seven children born in poverty to William and Laura Smith in Chattanooga, Tennessee, in 1894. Orphaned early, she was raised by her oldest sister, Viola. They were so poor that Bessie began earning her living on the streets of Chattanooga by singing.

In 1912, Ma Rainey's Rabbit Foot Minstrels came through town, and by the time their run in Chattanooga had ended, Bessie had joined the traveling show. She sang her way through the South, in dingy bars and rundown theaters. In 1920, she married Earl Love, but he died soon after the marriage and, in 1922, she married John Gee, a night watchman, in Philadelphia. After a rocky seven-year marriage, which included the adoption of a child and his unsuccessful management of her career, they separated.

Meanwhile, the recording director for Columbia Records, had heard Smith and decided to record her. In 1923, after her first recording session, Bessie's deep contralto voice, in blues and jazz renditions, made her a star. When she signed an exclusive contract with Columbia, the record company was teetering on the brink of bankruptcy. Bessie Smith's records are credited with saving Columbia during a difficult time in the record industry. As many as 100,000 of her records were sold in a week. This Bessie Smith craze earned her the title "Empress of the Blues."

In her career, she recorded 160 songs. This popularity brought her an impressive salary. She was able to star in her own traveling troupe of performers. Audiences, both Blacks and Whites, were drawn to her magnetic style. Among the songs that kept audiences returning were: *Weeping Willow Blues, Backwater Blues, Jazzbo Brown from Memphis Town, Cakewalking Babies, Gin House Blues,* and *Me and My Gin.* Her interpretation of popular tunes, *Aggravatin' Papa,* and *Baby, Won't You Please Come Home?* brought the crowds to their feet. Louis Armstrong, James P. Johnson, Charlie Green, and Joe Smith were among the music legends who accompanied her. At the peak of her career, in 1929, she appeared in the movie, *St. Louis Blues,* where she displayed her versatility as an actress.

Smith's star was shining brilliantly until 1933, when the blues craze began to fade. Her career then faltered, and she had to literally sing for her supper. Her earnings dwindled almost to nothing. On September 26, 1937, Bessie Smith was heading toward Memphis when, near Coahoma, Mississippi, her car collided with a parked panel truck and flipped over. Her arm was nearly severed. A doctor who happened to be on the scene tried to help until an ambulance arrived. In a hospital, her arm was amputated, but she died anyway, apparently of internal injuries. Although 7,000 people attended her funeral near Philadelphia, her grave remained without a marker for more than 30 years. A letter to a Philadelphia newspaper launched a campaign that rectified this omission.

Bessie Smith left an impressive legacy as an inspiration to such musical heavyweights as Billie Holliday and gospel singer Mahalia Jackson. In fact, Jackson often talked about how she would sneak away to a New Orleans theater to hear, in person, the woman who was a tremendous influence on her musical career—Bessie Smith.

HENRY OSSAWA TANNER
1859 -1937

American art as an independent force, not merely an offshoot of European art, got a significant boost from Henry Ossawa Tanner, the first Black artist of international fame. His success in Paris was unprecedented for a Black artist.

Tanner was born on June 21, 1859, in Pittsburgh, the oldest of seven children, born to Benjamin Tucker Tanner, a college graduate and a minister, and Sarah Elizabeth Tanner. When he was just barely into his teens, he developed a talent for art. His parents initially encouraged him, but fearing racism would block his ambitions, they later tried unsuccessfully to discourage him.

From 1876 to 1880, he painted portraits, landscapes, seascapes, and animals. Two of his landscapes, painted while he was in the Adirondacks, were exhibited at the Pennsylvania Academy of Fine Arts. After two years as a student at that school, he dropped out to make a living at his craft.

While he sold his etchings to such publications as *Harper's Young People* and saw his work exhibited at the Pennsylvania Academy of Fine Arts, and the National Academy of Design in New York, Tanner experienced only moderate financial success. So, on January 4, 1891, he went to Europe to study and have a life less ruled by racial discrimination.

After attending several prestigious art schools, in 1894, Tanner scored his first artistic triumph with his painting, *The Music Lesson.* The painting won acclaim and was accepted by the Societe des Artistes Francaise. Other paintings, *Daniel in the Lions Den* and *The Raising of Lazarus,* which was displayed in the Luxembourg Galleries in 1897, also won awards.

Tanner visited the Holy Land and regions of Europe, so he could gain first-hand knowledge of the area of his religious subjects. In 1898, his newly-painted creation, *Annunciation,* was acquired by and exhibited in the Philadelphia Museum.

Another trip to Palestine resulted in the painting *Christ and Nicodemus,* which was exhibited in Paris. On December 14, 1899, Tanner married Jessie Macauley Olssen, who had posed as Mary for his *Annunciation.* After their marriage, they had one son, Jesse Ossawa.

From 1900 to 1914, Tanner strengthened his reputation in Paris with such paintings as *Christ at Emmaus, Foolish Virgins,* and *The Two Disciples at the Tomb.* In 1905, he was the first Black American artist to have his work featured in the annual exhibition of the Carnegie Institute. In 1913, he was elected president of the Societe Aristique de Picardie and, during this period, he captured a series of honors for his artistic contributions.

The onset of World War I prompted Tanner to paint some war scenes, but they were executed without his usual inspiration. Nevertheless, at war's end, he was named chevalier of the Legion of Honor by the French government, one of his highest honors. And, in 1925, his painting, *Sodom and Gomorrah,* was exhibited at the Metropolitan Museum in New York. This was followed by more honors, including election to full membership in the prestigious National Academy in 1927.

In 1925, his wife died and his son's health began to fade. In the economic depression of the 1930s, Tanner was forced to move to a small apartment in Paris, where he occasionally painted until he, too, died on May 25, 1937. At first, his name was kept alive by a few Black writers. Since the 1960s, however, his works have received renewed interest. This came about because of public acceptance of Tanner's style of painting and the achievements of Blacks in general.

Star billing, the best theaters, and a handsome salary, Bert Williams earned them all. And, he led the way for other Blacks to earn the same. Williams was the first Black entertainer to star in the Ziegfeld Follies, the top theatrical production of the day.

With his pantomime routines, his humorous yet pathetic air, and his distinct singing and dancing, Bert Williams was tremendously popular. The ultimate compliment came from W.C. Fields, who said, "Williams was the funniest man I ever saw."

Williams was born Egbert Austin Williams in Providence, Nassau, in 1873. His formative years were spent on a Nassau plantation until his father died, and the family moved to California. Williams at first wanted to be an engineer, but he had no money for college. Because of his love of music, he learned to play several instruments, particularly the banjo. To earn money, he sang and danced in the streets. Eventually, he became a cafe entertainer in San Francisco.

In 1895, he met another Black comedian, George Nash Walker. The duo teamed up in an act that had Walker portraying the fast-talking slickster playing off of Williams' bumbling character. For 16 years, the two had audiences laughing all over the globe. For the Prince of Wales' ninth birthday, the pair was hired for a command performance at Buckingham Palace. They also appeared in such shows as *Sons of Ham* (1900), *In Dahomey* (1902), *In Abyssinia* (1908), and *Bandana Land!* (1908).

The team came to an abrupt end in 1907, when Walker fell ill and died soon afterward. Williams was forced to go solo and, after a series of moderate successes, the country's top theatrical producer, Florenz Ziegfeld, signed him to appear in the *Ziegfeld Follies* in 1910. This was a historic first for a Black; and for over a decade, he appeared in various Ziegfeld-produced shows and brought audiences to their feet with his routines. Williams was the hit of the shows. His trademark act came late in the show, when a white-gloved hand would appear followed by fingers moving in rhythm. Following, a long black-suited arm would emerge, next the other hand and arm, and finally Bert Williams, in blackface and in shabby clothes, in his full six-feet of comic splendor.

Despite his popularity, racism dogged him, and he often stayed in segregated hotels or took the freight elevator to his room in a Whites-only hotel. His contract stated that he would not appear on stage with a White woman, and that he would not perform in areas south of the Mason/Dixon line. He once remarked, "It is no disgrace to be a Negro, but it is inconvenient."

In addition to his theatrical fame, Williams made recordings that sold in the hundreds of thousands. They included such tunes as *Nobody; Jonah Man; I'm in the Right Church but the Wrong Pew; and Come After Breakfast, Bring Along Your Lunch and Leave Before Supper.* Adding to his versatility was his ability to dance. After his success with the *Ziegfeld Follies,* two shows were produced exclusively for him, *Broadway Brevities* (1920) and *Under the Bamboo Tree* (1922).

While performing in the latter production, Williams collapsed in a Detroit theater. After a bout with pneumonia, he died at age 47, leaving his wife, Lottie, and a world of admirers to mourn him. Although he performed in a disguise, hiding behind a mask of burnt cork, nothing could camouflage the talent of the man, the frowning and smiling clown facing the absurdities of everyday life.

NOTES

TEST YOURSELF

Now that you have familiarized yourself with our Historic Blacks in the Arts in this eighth series of Empak's Black History publications, this section, in three parts: MATCH; TRUE/FALSE; MULTIPLE CHOICE/FILL-IN, is designed to help you remember some key points about each notable Black in the Arts. (Answers on page 32)

MATCH

I. *Match the column on the right with the column on the left by placing the appropriate alphabetical letter next to the Historic Blacks in the Arts it represents.*

1. Marian Anderson _____
2. James Baldwin _____
3. Alexandre Dumas _____
4. Meta Vaux Warrick Fuller _____
5. Florence Mills _____
6. Bessie Smith _____
7. Bert Williams _____

A) "The Three Musketeers"
B) "Queen of the Blues"
C) Appeared in Blackface
D) Famed contralto
E) Author/playwright
F) Sculptress
G) Appeared in *Shuffle Along*

TRUE/FALSE

II. *The True and False statements below are taken from the biographical information given on each of the Historic Blacks in the Arts.*

1. Ira Frederick Aldridge was a great statesman who helped write the Emancipation Proclamation. _____
2. Josephine Baker gained fame as an entertainer at the famed Folies Bergere in Paris. _____
3. Thomas Green Bethune was a musical genius who earned over $100,000 for his master. _____
4. Robert Nathaniel Dett popularized jazz and toured the nation with his band. _____
5. Henry Ossawa Tanner was a famous boxer. _____
6. Paul Robeson was an actor and singer who gained world fame through his on-stage characters. _____
7. Charles Dean Dixon was a symphony orchestra conductor who achieved his fame in Europe. _____

MULTIPLE CHOICE/FILL-IN

III. *Complete the statements below by underlining the correct name, or by filling-in the correct answer which you have read in the biographical sketches.*

1. (Alexandre Dumas, Alexander Pushkin, Robert Duncanson) was one of Russia's greatest poets.
2. (Justin Holland, Edward Kennedy Ellington, W. C. Handy) was a viable and vital musical composer and conductor whose compositions included "Take the A Train."
3. This sculptress made her mark in Europe and then returned to America where her creations of Black figures and Black themes won acclaim. She is (Marian Anderson, Black Patti, Meta Vaux Warrick Fuller).
4. Author of award winning play, *A Raisin in the Sun* is (Scott Joplin, Lorraine Hansberry, Langston Hughes).
5. This legendary tap dancer appeared in film with Shirley Temple, he is (Bert Williams, Bill "Bojangles" Robinson, Paul Robeson).
6. (Bessie Smith, Florence Mills, Sissieretta Jones) is known as the "Queen of the Blues."
7. His interpretations of landscapes through his paintings captivated the art world, he is (Henry Ossawa Tanner, Robert Duncanson, Joshua Johnston).

CROSSWORD PUZZLE

ACROSS

1. Noted symphony orchestra conductor
3. Shakespeare's Othello
6. Ragtime
7. Masterful painter of Biblical themes
10. "The Emperor Jones"
12. He gave the guitar a new dimension
16. "Black Patti"
19. Star of the famous Ziegfeld Follies
20. Composer of the *St. Louis Blues*
22. Well-known child prodigy on the piano
23. Internationally known big band leader

DOWN

2. Prolific sculptor for over seventy years
4. Fame minstrel performer
5. *Land of the Lotus Eaters*
8. Performed at New York's Metropolitan Opera
9. *To Be Young, Gifted and Black*
11. Once sold 100,000 records in a week
13. He wrote, *The Count of Monte Cristo*
14. Starred in the play, "Blackbirds of 1926"
15. Poet who received pardon from exile
17. Go tell it in the Mountain
18. Once wore a girdle of bananas
21. Composer brought Spirituals to life

WORDSEARCH

1. Ira Frederick Aldridge
2. Marian Anderson
3. Josephine Baker
4. James Baldwin
5. Thomas Green Bethune
6. R. Nathaniel Dett
7. Dean Dixon
8. Alexandre Dumas
9. Robert Duncanson
10. Duke Ellington
11. Meta Vaux Warrick Fuller
12. W.C. Handy
13. Lorraine Hansberry
14. Justin Holland
15. Langston Hughes
16. Scott Joplin
17. Sissieretta Jones
18. Florence Mills
19. Alexander Pushkin
20. Paul Robeson
21. Bill Bojangles Robinson
22. Bessie Smith
23. Henry Ossawa Tanner
24. Bert Williams

The names of our twenty-four HISTORIC BLACKS IN THE ARTS are contained in the diagram below. Look in the diagram of letters for the names given in the list. Find the names by reading FORWARD, BACKWARDS, UP, DOWN, and DIAGONALLY in a straight line of letters. Each time you find a name in the diagram, circle it in the diagram and cross it off on the list of names. Words often overlap, and letters may be used more than once.

```
C X T L B E N T R U N T T E D L E I N A H T A N R F M
I E L L T J R F R E D S A M U D E R D N A X E L A E A
S A M Y L A N G S T O N H U G H E S M A R C U S T Y R
R D X Z T M J U T R S M A I L L I W T R E B V A N N I
E N U H T E B N E E R G S A M O H T U G L C V K F T A
K P M U S S E O I T Y E L B M U R C D X N A A S T I N
A T J E L B B T S D N A L L O H N I T S U J S T U V A
B B N T Y A D G D J E R K Y U N R S L X P V X N S S N
E R O R R L H N B B X D V V E D S H W C H A N D Y E D
N H S H L D T I L N N O E O L M M A R X G N V T Y N E
I Q N U L W I L Q U T T S A V L R E E F N I X T Q O R
H D A N X I M L T L X N K O N R O O V I N L E O L J S
P A C O M N S E H D L C U N I D R L E T I P U N L A O
E N N S A S E E A R I C H C C F I C T E D O L Y I T N
S C U E S B I K T R Q Q K A K A T X T O M J R D M T V
O E D B H R S U E S U F F R O U S T O L V T A E E E U
J R T O E U S D S T U P E R N E S T I N S T E B D R L
L X R R D N E N N L R E N N A T A W A S S O Y R N E H
U G E L Y R B T L S H O N S E M P A K D E C K I L I K
C N B U F U N E S F L O R E N C E M I L L S V D D S I
K I O A Y R R E B S N A H E N I A R R O L L K X I S V
Y S R P M E S S Y N I K H S U P D E D N A X E L A I I
B I L L B O J A N G L E S R O B I N S O N P U S H S T
```

MATCH

1.–D	5.–G
2.–E	6.–B
3.–A	7.–C
4.–F	

TRUE/FALSE

1.–FALSE	5.–FALSE
2.–TRUE	6.–TRUE
3.–TRUE	7.–TRUE
4.–FALSE	

MULTIPLE CHOICE/FILL-IN

1.–ALEXANDER PUSHKIN
2.–EDWARD KENNEDY ELLINGTON
3.–META VAUX WARRICK FULLER
4.–LORRAINE HANSBERRY

5.–BILL "BOJANGLES" ROBINSON
6.–BESSIE SMITH
7.–ROBERT DUNCANSON

CROSSWORD PUZZLE

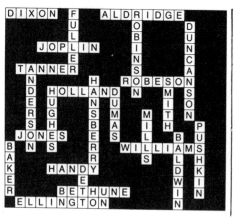

WORD SEARCH

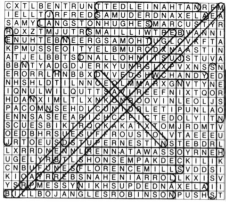

Name _____

Affiliation _____

Address _____
P. O. Box numbers not accepted, street address must appear.

City _____ State _____ Zip _____

Phone# (_____)_____ Date _____

Method Of Payment Enclosed:　( ) Check　　　( ) Money Order　　　( ) Purchase Order

Prices effective 11/1/96 thru 10/31/97

ADVANCED LEVEL

Quantity	ISBN #	Title Description	Unit Price	Total Price
	0-922162-1-8	"A Salute to Historic Black Women"		
	0-922162-2-6	"A Salute to Black Scientists & Inventors"		
	0-922162-3-4	"A Salute to Black Pioneers"		
	0-922162-4-2	"A Salute to Black Civil Rights Leaders"		
	0-922162-5-0	"A Salute to Historic Black Abolitionists"		
	0-922162-6-9	"A Salute to Historic African Kings & Queens"		
	0-922162-7-7	"A Salute to Historic Black Firsts"		
	0-922162-8-5	"A Salute to Historic Blacks in the Arts"		
	0-922162-9-3	"A Salute to Blacks in the Federal Government"		
	0-922162-14-X	"A Salute to Historic Black Educators"		

INTERMEDIATE LEVEL

	0-922162-75-1	"Historic Black Women"		
	0-922162-76-X	"Black Scientists & Inventors"		
	0-922162-77-8	"Historic Black Pioneers"		
	0-922162-78-6	"Black Civil Rights Leaders"		
	0-922162-80-8	"Historic Black Abolitionists"		
	0-922162-81-6	"Historic African Kings & Queens"		
	0-922162-82-4	"Historic Black Firsts"		
	0-922162-83-2	"Historic Blacks in the Arts"		
	0-922162-84-0	"Blacks in the Federal Government"		
	0-922162-85-9	"Historic Black Educators"		

Total Books			❸ Subtotal	
			❹ IL Residents add 8.75% Sales Tax	
	SEE ABOVE CHART ⟶		❺ Shipping & Handling	
GRADE LEVEL: 4th, 5th, 6th			❻ Total	

BOOK PRICING ● QUANTITY DISCOUNTS

Advanced Level	Intermediate Level
Reg. $3.49	Reg. $2.29
Order 50 or More	Order 50 or More
Save 40¢ EACH	Save 20¢ EACH
@ $3.09	@ $2.09

❺ SHIPPING AND HANDLING

Order Total	Add
Under $5.00	$1.50
$5.01-$15.00	$3.00
$15.01-$35.00	$4.50
$35.01-$75.00	$7.00
$75.01-$200.00	10%
Over $201.00	6%

In addition to the above charges, U.S. territories, HI & AK, add $2.00. Canada & Mexico, add $5.00. Other outside U.S., add $20.00.

Name _____

Affiliation _____

Street _____
P. O. Box numbers not accepted, street address must appear.

City _____ **State** _____ **Zip** _____

Phone (_____**)** _____ **Date** _____

Method Of Payment Enclosed: ( ) Check   ( ) Money Order   ( ) Purchase Order

Prices effective 11/1/96 thru 10/31/97

PRIMARY LEVEL... KINDERGARTEN, FIRST, SECOND & THIRD GRADE

Quantity	ISBN #	Title Description	Unit Price	Total Price
	0-922162-90-5	"Kumi and Chanti"		
	0-922162-91-3	"George Washington Carver"		
	0-922162-92-1	"Harriet Tubman"		
	0-922162-93-X	"Jean Baptist DuSable"		
	0-922162-94-8	"Matthew Henson"		
	0-922162-95-6	"Bessie Coleman"		
Total Books			❸ Subtotal	
			❹ IL Residents add 8.75% Sales Tax	
	SEE CHART BELOW ▷		❺ Shipping & Handling	
			❻ Total	

KEY STEPS IN ORDERING

❶ Establish quantity needs.   ❹ Add tax, if applicable.
❷ Determine book unit price.   ❺ Add shipping &handling.
❸ Determine total cost.   ❻ Total amount.

BOOK PRICING ● QUANTITY DISCOUNTS

❶ Quantity Ordered	❷ Unit Price
1-49	$3.49
50 +	$3.09

❺ SHIPPING AND HANDLING

Order Total	Add
Under $5	$1.50
$5.01-$15.00	$3.00
$15.01- $35.00	$4.50
$35.01-$75.00	$7.00
$75.01-$200.00	10%
Over $201.00	6%

In addition to the above charges, U.S. territories, HI & AK, add $2.00. Canada and Mexico, add $5.00. Other outside U.S., add $20.00.

Empak Publishing provides attractive counter and floor displays for retailers and organizations interested in the Heritage book series for resale. Please check here ☐ and include this form with your letterhead and we will send you specific information and our special volume discounts.

- The Empak "Heritage Kids" series provides a basic understanding and appreciation of Black history which translates to cultural awareness, self-esteem, and ethnic pride within young African-American children.

- Assisted by dynamic and impressive 4-color illustrations, readers will be able to relate to the two adorable African kids -- Kumi & Chanti, as they are introduced to the inspirational lives and deeds of significant, historic African-Americans.

Black History Materials
Available from Empak Publishing

A Salute To Black History Poster Series
African-American Experience–Period Poster Series
Biographical Poster Series
Heritage Kids Poster Series

Advanced Booklet Series
Instructor's Manuals
Advanced Skills Sheets
Black History Bulletin Board Aids
Instructor's Kits

Intermediate Booklet Series
Teacher's Guides
Intermediate Skill Sheets
Black History Flashcards
Intermediate Reading Certificates
Teacher's Kits

Heritage Kids Booklet Series
Heritage Kids Resource & Activity Guides
Heritage Kids Reading Certificates
Heritage Kids Kits

Black History Videos
Black History Month Activity & Resource Guide
African-American Times–A Chronological Record
African-American Discovery Board Game
African-American Clip Art
Black History Mugs
Black Heritage Marble Engraving
Black History Month Banners (18" x 60")
Say YES to Black History Education Sweatshirts
Say YES to Black History Education T-Shirts

To receive your copy of the Empak Publishing Company's
colorful new catalog, please send $2 to cover postage and handling to:

Empak Publishing Company
Catalog Dept., Suite 300
212 East Ohio Street
Chicago, IL 60611